Behind Media

Radio

Catherine Chambers

Heinemann
LIBRARY

www.heinemann.co.uk/library

Visit our website to find out more information about **Heinemann Library** books.

To order:
☎ Phone 44 (0) 1865 888066
🖹 Send a fax to 44 (0) 1865 314091
💻 Visit the Heinemann Bookshop at www.heinemann.co.uk/library to browse our catalogue and order online.

First published in Great Britain by Heinemann Library, Halley Court, Jordan Hill, Oxford, OX2 8EJ,
a division of Reed Educational and Professional Publishing Ltd.
Heinemann is a registered trademark of Reed Educational and Professional Publishing Ltd.

OXFORD MELBOURNE AUCKLAND
JOHANNESBURG BLANTYRE GABORONE
IBADAN PORTSMOUTH NH (USA) CHICAGO

Designed by Paul Davies and Associates
Originated by Ambassador Litho Ltd.
Printed in Hong Kong/China

ISBN 0 431 11462 5
05 04 03 02 01
10 9 8 7 6 5 4 3 2 1

British Library Cataloguing in Publication Data

Chambers, Catherine
  Radio. - (Behind Media)
  1.Radio - Juvenile literature
  I.Title
  791.4'4

Acknowledgements

The Publisher would like to thank the following for permission to reproduce photographs: Action-Plus/Glyn Kirk: p22; Arena:
pp4, 26, 30; Capital FM Radio: pp15, 17; Corbis: Christopher Cormack p32, The Purcell Team p6, Bob Rowan p13, Staffan
Widstrand p24; David Swindells: p40; Eliot Stein: p45; Environmental Images/Michael Marchant: p37; John Mead/Science
Photo Library: p34; Panos Pictures: p9, Crispin Hughes p8, Clive Shirley p21, Chris Stowers p38; Popperfoto: p41; Press
Association/Neil Munns: p19; Radio 4ZzZ: p10; Redferns/Suzi Gibbons: p19; Rex Features: p14; Science & Society Picture
Library/Science Museum: p44; Stay Still Ltd/Sven Arnstein: p39; Stone: p42; Sylvia Pitcher Photo Library: p11; Telegraph
Colour Library: pp16, 29; The Stock Market: p7; Tommy Hindley/Professional Sport: p5.

Cover photograph reproduced with permission of Telegraph Colour Library.

Our thanks to Robert McLeish for his comments in the preparation of this book.

Every effort has been made to contact copyright holders of any material reproduced in this book.
Any omissions will be rectified in subsequent printings if notice is given to the Publisher.

Contents

The Waves at Daybreak

Getting it off the Ground

The Show Begins

All in a Day's Work

Behind the Mike

Turn the Radio On

Any words appearing in the text in bold, **like this**, are explained in the Glossary.

The Waves at Daybreak

Why radio?

About 80 years ago, switches were clicked, knobs were turned and like magic, plain wooden boxes suddenly sparked into life. At first muffled and crackled, real voices crossed invisible waves and entered the heart of the home. In a short space of time, radio became an entertainer, an educator and a companion for billions of people all over the world.

Radio stations around the globe wake us every morning with news, views, music and chat. This book aims to take you through an early-morning radio show, explaining how it is put together and broadcast to a local community. But other shows and aspects of radio broadcasting will feature too, to give you a wider picture of this medium.

*DJs, newsreaders, weather reporters and **continuity** announcers all have to interact with perfect timing to create entertaining and interesting programmes. Often, a newsreader or special guest will record in a separate studio from the main presenter.*

What is the attraction?

A radio can be portable, and it is cheap. It can be listened to quietly through headphones or it can be enjoyed by a whole roomful of people. You can drive and listen at the same time. You can walk, work and listen, too. Recent research has found that you can even revise for your exams with your favourite pop station on and it will actually help you!

Radio can be tuned in to at any time of the day and night – there will always be something to keep the listener company. He or she can even tune in to a station abroad and help brush up their foreign languages. Without pictures, the listener's imagination can run riot, too.

These are just some of the reasons why, in the USA, people listen to the radio for an average of three hours every day. And it is why the USA now has over 14,000 radio stations. World-wide, the scale of radio is enormous. UNESCO (United Nations Educational, Scientific and Cultural Organization) estimates that there are 2.4 billion radio sets throughout the world. And of all the thousands of stations across the globe, local stations are considered to be the heart and soul of the radio broadcasting industry, bringing the community into the home and the workplace.

Specialist stations offer specialist news. Sports stations provide the latest information on clubs, players and transfers – the financial side of sports as well as the trials, trophies and gossip. They also use specialist presenters, such as John McEnroe for tennis.

Who makes it all happen?

Radio personalities are the most hidden of all the media world. The listener rarely sees who creates the programmes – and rarely does he or she recognize them when they pick up their trophies at broadcasting awards' ceremonies. But behind the scenes a team of **producers**, **directors**, production assistants, **studio managers**, editors and technicians mould voices and noises into shape. This book will look at the functions of many of those involved in radio production, the techniques they use and the workings of a recording studio.

Will it last?

Since the 1950s, radio has met fierce competition from television. When TV first appeared, radio **ratings** plummeted and producers were forced to think of new ways of attracting an audience. Teenagers came to the rescue with their thirst for popular music and culture, and so the pop station was born. Later, we shall see how radio is holding up against the latest media development – the Internet.

What's the story?

The expression '**drive time** is **prime time**' describes how most people listen in to news and views between 6.30 and 9.30 am – a time when many are on their way to work. Every day countless radio and television stations vie for their share of the early morning audience. What does radio have to offer?

Morning glory

If you flick through the radio channels around breakfast time you will find a great range of early morning shows. In the last 30 years these have established a strong identity in the face of competition from breakfast television. But while television provides a very accessible account of news, comment and entertainment, it tends to stress the big national and international events. These are often of greater visual impact than the smaller stories or local news. Natural disaster, war, accident, crime, political scandal and glitzy awards ceremonies are all standard television material. But for the early-morning commuter they are only a background for the more important task ahead – how to get to work on time, armed with enough information about what is going on locally and in the world at large. It is time to tune in to the radio.

On the pulse

Radio can provide people getting ready to face the day with all the information they require: the national and international headlines, regional news items, financial updates and frequent time checks. National and regional weather forecasts, and often traffic news, help the travelling listener to prepare for the conditions they may encounter.

Most traffic news is supplied by reporters using helicopters to track trouble spots. Together with information from the emergency services and road maintenance companies they keep the commuter well informed. Many traffic bulletins include suggested road diversions.

*Prime-time hours are defined through extensive market research undertaken by broadcasters and **ratings** companies. They use a variety of techniques to gauge the listening habits of radio fans such as these.*

Radio manages to communicate information in a few set **formats**. Presentation ranges from pop shows interrupted by quick news bulletins, to straightforward news summaries followed by lengthy analysis. Some stations are known for their serious content and tone, while others pick out off-beat stories and present them in an amusing way. So you can pick your station to suit your mood as well as your needs. On commercial stations, advertisements and **jingles** break the serious moments or the musical monotony.

Out of the ark

In the last two decades, early-morning pop and chat shows have adopted the 'zoo' formula – a mad concoction of lively presenters, co-presenters and media personalities. The contents include very informal chat with listeners on bizarre subjects, wild antics in the studio – oh, and the occasional news bulletin! This formula began in the USA and has spread to many corners of the world. While it is still very popular, one ex-prime-time presenter, Noel Edmonds, has said of the 'zoo formula', '...I think that radio is an intimate medium from one person to another. You can get the feeling that if there is a group of people on the radio they are having a better time than you are and there are in-jokes that you don't understand that unsettle you.' What do you think of the debate?

Early radio

✿ From the 1920s, **producers** realized that listening to the news was a much quicker and more convenient way of catching up with events than reading the newspaper.

✿ In 1922, Radio 2LO became the British Broadcasting Company's first London station. One of the first items was the news. It was read twice, once at normal speed and once very slowly. Each news item was separated from the next by a chime of tubular bells – supposed to be a chiming clock!

Wide horizons

Radio is a web of information that spirals outwards from local stations to international networks. It has long been used to educate at both levels. How does this work in different parts of the world?

Listen and learn

Radio has always been used to inform and educate both adults and young people. In many areas, its role for the young has been largely to supplement classroom teaching, often using plays, music, stories and games to encourage learning. In more remote parts of the world, radio has been used for communicating the mainstream school syllabus. Some local radio stations serve ethnic minority communities, providing news and entertainment in a variety of languages. But their contacts are world-wide, tapping into reports from the original 'home' country and other parts of the world where people of the same community have settled.

In rural areas, local radio helps farmers to keep up with developments in agriculture. Internationally, the BBC World Service's 'Farming World' programme discusses global agricultural techniques. Many stations are now linked to websites so that hard-working farmers can study the information in their own time.

In a more tragic setting, radio is playing a big part in rehabilitating Rwanda's children following the massacres in 1998. These left many children without parents and many households with an older brother or sister in charge of younger siblings. In 2000, the Rwandan government and the charity, War Child, set about providing a radio service which aims to educate all Rwanda's children whose schools have not yet been rebuilt, focusing especially on the young carers. These students will be given not only mainstream education but also information on childcare, immunization programmes and farming techniques, for these children are also the family providers. War Child is providing 65,000 BayGen Freeplay radios which work without batteries or mains electricity (see also page 45).

*One of the most successful and longest-running education projects has been Australia's School of the Air, which operates in very inaccessible, sparsely populated rural areas. With regular broadcast lessons, and tutorials on **two-way radio**, farming families have been able to educate their children. In recent years, the Internet has supplemented this with e-mail communication.*

Radio sets around the world

This table gives an idea of the number of radio sets listened to in different countries. It is not always necessarily true that the richer the nation, the more radio sets per person. Television is usually the preferred medium in wealthier countries.

There is a lot of interdependence between local, national and international radio broadcasting. But the quality and variety of information used depends a lot on how the station is financed.

Country	Population (in millions)	No. of radio sets on average
Australia	19	1.4 per person
France	59	1 per person
India	944	1.2 per 10 people
Italy	57	8.8 per 10 people
Nigeria	115	1 per 5 people
UK	59	1.4 per person
USA	275	More than 2 per person

Radio power

Many of the world's most powerful nations broadcast to as many countries as possible through publicly-funded international stations. The Voice of America is the foreign broadcasting arm of the United States; the BBC World Service, that of the United Kingdom. Some of their programmes subtly promote their own political and financial interests abroad. Others give listeners an insight into projects and developments throughout the world. However, the BBC has built its reputation on reporting 'truth' even when it is not in Britain's interest. Both stations have also been used for intelligence purposes, especially during times of conflict.

Getting it off the Ground

Paying the piper

How does a new programme get off the ground? Well, let us start with the nitty-gritty subject of money! Every programme has to be financed, which means that it has to have a proven need and a target audience before it will find any backers. Radio programmes can be funded in a number of ways, including commercial advertising, licence fees, subscription and government funding.

Who is listening?

Densely populated urban areas spawn a large number of radio stations with a huge following. There is a lot of competition for both listeners and **revenue**. Rural areas, being sparsely populated, generate less revenue than urban areas and can sustain only a few local stations.

Bananas and microphones do go together – well, at least in Queensland, Australia they do. They represent the state's controversial 25-year-old radio station 'Triple-Z'. It has financed itself by various means, including a 'Zedbubble' Market Day and this message to encourage sponsorship; 'Zed has over 100 dedicated volunteers working their butts off so we can stay on air.'

Many costs of running stations are roughly the same for all areas, depending on the size and number of their studios rather than their location. These include power, equipment, licences, telephone and satellite links – basically, all the required equipment and services that are bought outright or hired. The salaries of technical personnel, too, are similar for all stations. **Prime-time** radio presenters, on the other hand, can command huge fees, especially those employed on national radio located in major cities. City premises are also expensive to buy or rent.

Finding the money

Commercials or advertisements account for most of a local commercial station's revenue. A lot of advertising time is bought by local retailers and service industries. Station advertising representatives (reps) also negotiate with national advertising companies and promotions departments of multi-national companies to sell **air time**. However, while these national **network** contracts can be lucrative, they must not overwhelm local advertising. A local station cannot afford to lose its loyal listener base. Both local and national commercial stations lure sponsorship for individual programmes or even small **slots** within them, such as quizzes, as well as for the station as a whole. Internet radio is now attracting huge amounts of investment. In May 2000, USA **Digital** Radio, based in Maryland, received $41 million to develop its world-wide service.

Capturing the audience

The formula for radio shows is continually being re-evaluated, especially the prime-time breakfast show. There are often slight changes in presentation or presenter, which freshen the image without costing a great deal or losing the regular, dedicated listener. These changes are often timed for the beginning of the new year – and the birth of the millennium saw a huge number of revamped radio shows. But when a new programme completely replaces an old one, it usually means that the slot or even the whole station has suffered a drop in the **ratings**.

A small rural station like this may have fewer premises and staff costs than a city station – but also generates far less income.

Ratings affect the profitability of all radio stations, however they are financed. For example, some governments support national radio stations solely or partially by collecting taxes or imposing a licence fee. But they cannot justify an increase in these unless the station's programmes are popular. Independent sponsors, such as financial institutions or manufacturers, do not want their name associated with a failing station or individual programme. Advertising agencies will not risk their clients' confidence by buying an unpopular slot. The clients themselves watch ratings very carefully before they part with money to promote their product or service. Popularity, therefore, is the most crucial factor in a station's profit margins.

The nation's stations

Every country regulates its broadcasting industry and provides a framework within which radio stations have to work. This includes their finance structure, granting licences so that stations can operate, and allocating them **wavebands** (see also page 39).

Radio arrangements

The way radio is arranged depends a lot on how each nation itself is structured, in terms of how it is divided into metropolitan districts, counties or states. It also depends on the political and economic system, and communications policies.

In some countries, as well as national and local rural or city stations, there are also regional, state and county stations. These reflect regional culture and broader interests and issues than those of local radio. This counteracts the rather 'capital-city' flavour of national stations. Regional radio is often publicly funded – an arm of national public radio, where that exists.

In Communist countries such as China, all media are government controlled, even regarding content. In recent years, however, there has been a loosening of the tight rein held on radio by officials. In most other countries, government broadcasting regulations cover all stations, no matter how they are funded. Regulatory bodies can enforce policies by fining radio stations or removing their licences. These bodies can control content to a certain extent, too. One of the most worrying issues for the USA's Federal Communications Commission (FCC) is that commercial radio does not fulfil its public obligations – that is, broadcast enough news, public health and weather warnings, and traffic and travel information and advice. Another issue is piracy – copying broadcast material. This has become more pressing with the development of Internet **digital** radio, which can be easily copied to a high standard.

A voice for all

Most **democratic** nations try to encourage an independent voice in broadcasting. Even many tax-funded systems make sure of this by using the money to create a public broadcasting authority which is free of government control, while still following broadcasting guidelines. The Netherlands has developed a complex broadcasting system. It not only allows an independent voice but also tries to take account of the country's diverse multicultural and multi-faith society.

Under the Media Act of 1988, two national organizations in the Netherlands co-ordinate broadcasting – an independent group of businesses that provides production facilities, and a joint government and private sector company that **transmits** most programmes of general interest. These programmes are produced by non-profit-making units that represent different interest groups – religious, artistic and loosely political, although not of any particular political party. Each group is funded through taxing the nation's five million radio owners. The amount of money that each group receives depends on the number of its members.

*Many small local stations represent minority interests and organizations, including unusual stations such as the USA's 'Focus on the Family' radio theatre, which broadcasts plays. This specialist transmission is known as **narrowcasting** and includes university and hospital radio stations, which are run on a shoestring, often with a lot of voluntary staff.*

In Australia and the UK

Ninety per cent of Australia's population owns a radio set. The publicly-funded Australian Broadcasting Corporation operates about 240 radio stations across the nation's states and territories. But Australia also licences 140 commercial stations funded by advertising and sponsorship. In the UK, over 95 per cent of households owns a radio set. The British Broadcasting Corporation is funded by a licence fee paid by the public. As well as this there is a thriving private sector which, through advertising and sponsorship, funds national and local radio stations.

Who is in control?

The radio **producer** and **director** run individual radio programmes. Unlike for most television and film productions, the producer and director are often the same person. But in most stations they cannot work alone. Nor do they take sole responsibility for the broadcast.

The scheme of things

There is huge diversity in the way radio stations are managed. It all depends on the size of the station, how much money is available and the nature of the funding. In very small stations run on a shoestring, the owner, programme planner and producer are often the same person. The content of their output (what is **transmitted**) is limited and so, often, are the hours of broadcasting.

The owner of a radio station has the ultimate responsibility for output and to a certain extent shapes its artistic and political content. The owners of national stations or **networks** are usually powerful multimedia people. They are rarely seen or heard, unlike owners of very small, independent local stations. A radio **station manager** is in charge of finances and makes sure that there is enough commercial sponsorship or public funding to sustain the right quantity and variety of programming. He or she is also responsible for what is broadcast from day to day. Programme planners and producers set the schedule, working out which programmes will fill the **slots** and determining the content. For commercial stations, they also allocate a certain amount of targeted advertising for each slot. The director for each programme makes sure that each item is broadcast to the best effect and on time.

Interactive radio slots attract money as well as good ratings. Radio phone-in, fax and e-mail discussions and quizzes allow people to participate. They are extremely popular and generate a big audience.

Control, cash and content

Programme structuring, scheduling and content is affected by methods and amounts of funding, **ratings**, trends and ownership. Advertising, or the lack of it, is a crucial factor in programme-planning and content. Publicly-financed programmes are not usually broken up by commercials. Some listeners like the smooth, uninterrupted programming that this produces. Others find it lacks sparkle. Advertisements can inject bursts of humour and music.

Ratings affect the type of breakfast show broadcast. To obtain ratings, research is conducted to work out the likely number and type of listeners at particular times of the day. These in turn affect the station's daily programme schedule. Each programme is targeted at a particular audience, based on age, income, ethnic origin, social background, and so on. In the last 20 years, top-rated programmes have been copied by producers of both local stations and national networks. This has led to a lack of variety, particularly among pop stations. Commenting on the UK's Sony Radio Awards (2000), UK journalist Anne Karpf stated: 'Commercial radio, much of which is owned by a trio of large groups, is so **formatted** that innovation is a foreign word.' The sameness is relieved only when a station is bold enough to try something new. But successful 'novelties' are always copied, making everything stale again!

Radio roadshows take music and chat around the country. Many pop radio stations also sponsor local or national pop concerts. Free tickets, invitations to talk to the presenters and musicians, and live acoustic 'jam' sessions are all part of the package.

On the job

A station manager needs to know about finance in the media, and have a good working knowledge of all aspects of radio production. He or she needs to have a good relationship with advertisers, radio producers and presenters alike. Many station managers begin as producers for local radio, learning the type of advertisement or sponsorship needed for each slot.

The Show Begins

In the studio

Forget glamour – radio studios are usually small, claustrophobic and totally lacking in luxury! This is especially true of local stations on a small budget. But enthusiastic **directors**, presenters and **audio technicians** can use the limited space and complex equipment to broadcast a seamless show.

Small is beautiful

Many local stations, particularly those used in colleges, hospitals or other **narrowcast** organizations, **transmit** from a single room. While this means that production noise is difficult to get rid of, especially during a live show, modern technology is making it possible to produce a professional programme in an ever-shrinking space. Even larger, national radio stations sometimes use single studios for a number of live programmes, especially pop music shows.

However, some programmes, especially news ones, use two rooms – a talks studio and a control room that is set behind a large window. Both are soundproofed. The talks studio allows for live, in-studio interviews and discussions between several people rather than just phone-ins. There are several advantages to this. The discussion is more focused and is usually deeper as the participants talk face to face. The presenter has more control over the proceedings and there is less likelihood of technical hiccups and poor sound quality which phone-ins sometimes generate. The **producer**/director co-ordinates the programme from the control room, while the **studio manager (SM)** handles the technical side. This means controlling **fades**, **cues** and pre-recorded material, such as the **signature tune** and pre-recorded interviews.

*These long sliders on the mixing desk are called **faders**. Every sound channel that leads from a microphone has its own fader, which is used to bring the sound in and then fade it up, down or out. The SM uses these to balance sound, to end items and cue music, sound effects and new items.*

The talks studio often consists of just a table, chairs, microphones, headphones and sound channel leads wired into the control room. In the control room, sound from the microphones is balanced by the SM at the mixing desk. In a talks situation, many interviewees are inexperienced in microphone technique – their voice is sometimes too soft, but more often, too loud. The SM tries to compensate for this by decreasing the input from their microphone. But there is not much that can be done about dead air – an often unexplainable silence caused by technical hitches.

Before the broadcast

Although early morning shows are live, there is a lot of preparation beforehand. For a new show, many pre-recorded items have to be made or chosen, ranging from signature tunes, through **jingles** to local commercials. Before the show goes on air, the producer and SM have to make sure that all the equipment is there and in working order. Pre-recorded tapes and music CDs are put in playing order. Tape cartridges holding the jingles are ready to plug in. The scripts for the day's news items are prepared on screen – most studios are now equipped with a computer monitor. Microphone levels are taken – if more than one is being used, the SM makes sure that the sound coming through them is balanced. The presenter appears about 45 minutes before going on air to have another look at the schedule and the material.

The producer or director, and the studio manager, arrive in the studio before the presenter. There is a lot of equipment to be checked and set up, and a seamless show requires careful preparation beforehand.

Setting the schedule

For our purposes, the local station operates as part of a commercial **network**, which owns national as well as other local stations. This gives us an opportunity to take a look at a wide range of material and commercial issues surrounding a broad spectrum of '**drive-time**' shows.

The early bird...

The first decision the programme planner needs to make is what is the best time to run the programme. A lot depends on the competition. **Prime time**, as we have seen, is about 6.30 to 9.30 am. But in many major cities more and more people are leaving for work early – a large number commute from suburbs or rural areas. Life is tougher – working hours are longer and people start out earlier. In response to this, many breakfast shows now begin at 6 am, when people are preparing for the day ahead. A station wishing to freshen its image with a new breakfast show might consider starting even earlier to catch the first listeners of the morning. From then on, it is a tussle with other stations to hold the listeners' attention with information and entertainment. A new breakfast show **format** might begin something like this:

5.45   Voice over faded-down catchy new **signature tune** – presenter of previous **slot** leads into the new breakfast show, introduces the recently-signed **freelance** presenter, tells everyone how wonderful he or she is, reminds listeners of the time and signs off. (30 seconds)
        Cue commercial for a major chain of coffee houses. (30 seconds)
5.46   Cue brief news bulletin. (15 seconds)
        Cue local weather update including airport, road and rail conditions. (15 seconds)
        Cue travel update including accidents, roadworks and reinforcing weather conditions affecting road, rail and air. (15 seconds)
        Fade in and up new signature tune again and fade down into presenter of new breakfast show who reminds listeners of the time, fades out the signature tune, introduces him or herself and leads into a chart record. (15 seconds)

...gets to work on time

So in just two minutes the listeners know that something different is happening on the station. They are updated with news, weather and travel and they are reminded that they can break their journey with a stop-off at a coffee house. They are also alerted to what time it is, a feature that continues throughout the prime-time show. This is a very important part of holding on to listeners in a hurry. As a safety issue, it stops drivers from continually looking at their clocks.

So far, the schedule is running exactly on time. But this show broadcasts pop music and local phone-in items as well as news and information. The length of tracks varies and interactive chats are unpredictable in length, so these tend to put out the schedule a little. News updates often do not occur exactly on the hour, or half-hour, but they are as near as possible. So, too, are commercial slots.

*DJs have access to hundreds of CDs. Most well-known pop stations have a music policy set out by a **producer** or **director**. DJs can only play a few CDs of their own choice.*

On the job

A DJ, or disc jockey, needs a smooth voice with a good low note and the ability to keep talking in a calm, confident but friendly way. They also have to be quick thinkers to make interesting links between different slots in the programme. A very good knowledge of commercial music and show business personalities is essential. Try working with a DJ at a school dance and start by taking a small slot in the programme. Most DJs begin in voluntary radio, then progress to local radio. Some have acting qualifications.

Live music is being played by a local musician on an early morning show. Guests have to be skilfully organized by the producer or director and the presenter, so that they do not run too much over time.

The full picture

Early morning shows are like eyes and ears for busy people. They try to give the listener a complete package of information – everything from a 'recipe for today', through to a handy hint for local evening entertainment. Occasionally their function is vital – radio can save lives!

Not in the schedule

The portability and accessibility of radio make it one of the best ways of contacting people in an emergency situation. In times of crisis, local, national and even international radio stations interrupt their schedule to make special calls to particular listeners asking them to contact their family or the police.

But sudden broadcasts are sometimes made on a much larger scale, alerting people to life-threatening emergency situations. In countries where there are many kinds of natural disaster, radio stations are linked to disaster warning systems. The USA and Japan in particular have developed close links with radio, particularly in their earthquake, hurricane, tornado and tsunami (tidal wave) zones. The USA also uses radio as part of its flood warning system. Instruments such as floodmetres and earthquake seismometers trigger warning systems at local stations.

Vital links

The US National Weather Center has permanently open emergency links with both television and radio, which interrupt their regular schedule when different levels of alert need to be broadcast. In Tornado Alley, a vast tract of southern and central USA, professional 'twister chasers' alert local weather centres and radio stations when tornado-bearing clouds begin to look dangerous. Radio warnings enable people living and working in the twister's path to seek safety in tornado shelters, while motorists have a chance to get out of their cars – one of the most dangerous places to be. Radio also plays an important part in smooth evacuation. It is rare, however, for the final tornado warning to occur in the middle of an early morning show, for most twisters strike in the late afternoon and early evening, just as workers are leaving their offices and factories. But the **prime-time** breakfast show is used to inform listeners that suspicious-looking clouds are on the way.

The final fade

Before the final **fade**, a prime-time show often leads the listener into the next programme with a **trail** – a short section of the item if it is pre-recorded, such as a play, or a descriptive introduction if it is live. The presenter will try to set you up for the rest of your day, ending on a cheerful note and reminding the listener of the evening's entertainment – not only on your radio station but also on television, at the movies, the theatre or on choice websites.

Later on in the day, the liveliest or most controversial moments of a prime-time breakfast show are rebroadcast, reminding loyal listeners what they will miss if they don't tune in the next day. These trails are also designed to encourage new listeners to switch from their regular station to a new one in those vital early-morning hours.

Countries with poor road, rail and air communications rely heavily on radio in an emergency situation. In a disaster situation, like the floods seen here in Somalia, two-way radio is often used to co-ordinate rescue teams and the distribution of emergency supplies. Local radio keeps dispersed, trapped and isolated people informed about the disaster and the relief effort.

Technical tips

Once an emergency warning has been broadcast, the presenter needs to bring the listener back into the programme with a snappy introduction or perhaps a **jingle**. Jingles and special effects are used especially on morning pop and 'zoo' shows to 'glue' items together as links and leads or break them up to jolt the listener. Effects can be pre-recorded inside or outside the studio and faded in from tapes. Noises like gushing water and echoes can also be held **digitally** and accessed by computer. Voice echo can be achieved by the 'echo mike' or synthesizer.

All in a Day's Work

Breaking the news

Producing news items throughout the day is a bit of a juggling act, and involves maintaining the main headlines of the morning yet breaking new stories as they occur. Some features, particularly updates of the world's money markets, are staple breakfast-news items. But by the early evening, many of the morning's headlines might just get brief mentions as the day's 'other stories'. In times of crisis, though, or during such events as elections, the headlines remain the same for several days. So, too, do the topics for discussion programmes that follow.

The listener to the local radio show expects to be familiar with the places and people they are hearing about. It is this familiarity that keeps a local audience tuned in and makes them feel part of the community, even if they have to leave it for the greater part of the day.

Sniffing out the story

'Headlines' and 'stories' are words taken from another news medium — the newspaper. Radio is not very different in its methods of collecting news items. Radio journalists are often **freelance** general journalists, also employed by newspapers and other media.

Radio takes advantage of on-the-spot coverage of events around the world, such as demonstrations, disasters, sports events, political rallies, ceremonies and elections. A good sports commentator enables the listener to visualize a sport through detailed description and lively presentation. This requires a lot of knowledge, especially for diverse sports carried out at world events such as the Olympic Games.

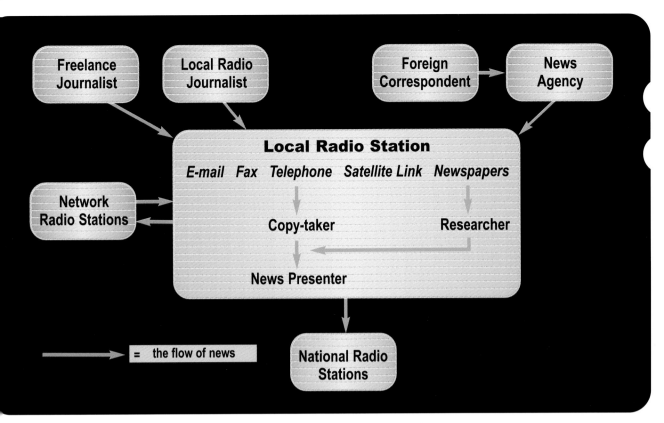

Freelance Journalist

Local Radio Journalist

Foreign Correspondent

News Agency

Local Radio Station

E-mail   Fax   Telephone   Satellite Link   Newspapers

Network Radio Stations

Copy-taker

Researcher

News Presenter

⟶ = the flow of news

National Radio Stations

This diagram shows how news flows into a local radio station. But you can see that some of it also flows out again to national radio stations, which rely on local networks to supply information on events occurring in remote parts of the country.

Many news items come second-hand, via other media. Or they are **network** items from other radio stations, some of which are pre-recorded overnight. Pop stations often present only brief bulletins with the occasional opinion thrown in by the DJ and listeners. They very rarely contain original material researched by their own journalists. To keep up-to-date with its stories, radio sometimes uses established news agencies such as Britain's Reuters, France's Agence France-Presse and America's Associated Press and United Press International.

Sending the story

For radio, all these stories are either sent to the station by e-mail or fax, or phoned in and taken down by a person called a copy-taker. With mobile phone and hand-held satellite communication systems, radio has become an immediate source of the latest information. Network radio stations can now share stories through computer systems interconnected by telephone lines. Live reporters have a limited time to give a rounded view of a situation – sometimes a mere phone call's-worth of facts, opinions and interviews. **Prime-time** radio listeners often tune in only to catch up with the main headlines and very basic issues surrounding them.

On the job

A radio journalist needs good research and writing skills and the ability to construct clear, concise reports suitable for the radio medium. He or she has to be able to communicate well with the public and people in high places alike. You could begin by writing news bulletins for your school newspaper and reading broadcasts for your local hospital or college radio. Make sure you tape any of your work that is broadcast. It can be used to build up a portfolio to present at interview.

Let's take a commercial break

Most **prime-time** shows are funded by sponsors and commercials – both local and national. The bulk of the commercials pay for the capital costs of a station and its permanent staff as well as for music royalties (payment paid to a band when its record is played). Special **slots** such as quizzes, advice sessions and phone-ins are often separately sponsored by businesses.

*How does 'invisible' radio advertise itself? Sometimes you will see T-shirts, car stickers and roadside signs promoting a particular station – and now there are radio advertisements on the Internet. But most of the advertising is carried out by presenters reminding you of whom you are listening to and which **waveband** you are tuned into.*

What is on offer?

Commercials are spoken advertisements – the term 'advertisement' usually refers to written ads, still images used in newspapers and magazines, or ads on billboards and hoardings. Radio commercials range from **jingles** and **voice-overs** lasting just a few seconds to half-minute and minute-long slots. These longer commercials are often dramatized.

Radio commercials advertise not only manufactured products and financial services but also charities and public initiatives such as drink-drive campaigns. Other types of information include paying taxes on time and party political broadcasts. Government-funded commercials like these are usually aired on both public and private radio stations. They are the only kind of commercial that many publicly-owned stations are allowed to run.

Election issues

Under the laws of most nations, presenters should give no opinion on a party political issue when an election is due. This includes local elections and referenda, like the 1999 Australian referendum on severing ties with the British monarchy, where each person in the country could vote yes or no. As we shall see on page 40, there are other restrictions placed on radio advertising.

The right slot

We have seen that the first commercial for the new breakfast show on Monday morning advertised a chain of coffee houses – a good time to plug their product. Finding suitable slots during the day or night and the right time of year is important – no one, for instance, wants to hear a commercial for central heating during a heat wave!

Unfortunately, however, the timing of commercials is not always under the programme scheduler's complete control. Prime-time radio, especially, can command high fees for its commercial slots, and an inappropriate product might just be the one that can pay the most money. However, it is not in the interests of a product manufacturer, service provider or radio station to put people off a brand by timing their commercials poorly. Internet radio has no need to break for advertisements – ad banners flash at you constantly at the side of the web page. Does this attract you – or irritate you?

Making the most of it

National holidays such as Australia Day or American Independence Day are exploited by radio presenters, product manufacturers and advertisers alike. So, too, are celebrations such as Christmas, Easter and Mother's Day. Saint Patrick's Day is also a target for commercials. In 2000, a product promoted for Saint Patrick's Day was readvertised for a mythical 'Saint Terry's Day' on the following Friday! This exploited the high profile of Saint Patrick's Day, extending the commercial's life-span very quickly and cheaply for another week.

Luring the listener

Radio commercials have to work very hard at attracting the listener. The writing and the acting have to compensate for the lack of visual image. Among the huge range of styles and production techniques it is often the element of surprise that makes people sit up and listen.

Simple or slick?

Local commercials are produced cheaply and often consist of short **jingles** with a simple **voice-over**. In small, local radio stations the voice-over may be performed live by the presenter or the DJ rather than pre-recorded by a separate announcer. These are usually not the most imaginative of commercials but they do nudge people into exploring local facilities.

National or **network** stations broadcast more commercials for well-known brands and labels. The commercials are either very slick or very wacky but in both cases cost more money to record. Actors perform small sketches – even miniature sitcoms that change every few weeks. Opposite is an imaginary script for a commercial. Try to guess what it is advertising before you reach the end. Do you think the commercial is pitched correctly for the product? You can read more about performing for radio on pages 28 and 30.

*Jingles are recorded to advertise not only goods and services but also the radio station's own **slots** and presenters. Short, sung jingles often get a message across more effectively than longer, more complex spoken advertisements, which require the listener to concentrate harder and longer.*

How do they do it?

The following fictitious commercial is technically quite simple, with the spoken word, few sound effects and no distracting background music or jingles. The commercial captures the listener's attention with its humour and by keeping the audience guessing as to which product is being advertised. In fact, this is how you would generally expect to see a radio commercial script – known as copy – set out, with instructions for the actor in square brackets and underlined. Instructions for the control room are written in capitals. This commercial, as with all others, has to be approved by an advertising standards authority before it can be broadcast.

> **FADE** IN AND UP
>
> ACTOR: [Dreamy, romantic and tortured, tapping frantically at a keyboard]
> Anna, oh Anna, wrenching my heart like an adjustable spanner.
> Er - spanner? ... Maybe not.
> [Sighs, deletes text and starts again]
> Your eyes gleam and glisten – stars in the sky,
> Moist and brown like a wet mud pie ...
> [Frustrated angst]
> No, NO – it just won't DO!
> [Creative, tortured voice]
> I am mesmerized by your magnetic face
> Because you look like something from outer ...
> (and here the listener is supposed to complete the rhyme with 'space'!)
> [Frustrated rage]
> Help me, Shakespeare, I just can't do it!
> FADE TO BLACK

*Jingles and advertisements are **cued** in by a DJ, using equipment such as a computer, or the cart machine (centre) and **faders** seen here.*

After the 'poet's' agonizing, a bright but sensible voice tells him he would be better off taking his loved one out for a candle-lit dinner than trying to write a love poem. So have we finally got to the the point of the commercial? No, not yet! It is not promoting a restaurant. Only at the end do we know the key product being advertised – a car-hire company specializing in luxury vehicles for that special journey. The car-hire company's name is then repeated by the calm voice-over to reinforce the brand in our minds.

Behind the Mike

Easy listening

It may all sound easy, but presenting and announcing on radio is very skilful. With live radio, the presenter always has to be prepared to react to the unexpected – a surprising news story, an irate listener, or even a blown fuse! But more than this, their voice must keep the audience tuned in.

It is all in the voice

Local radio lacks the resources for a large stable of presenters and **continuity** announcers. It relies on the vocal skills of a limited number to keep the listener interested. Whilst the clarity has to be maintained, so does variety in **pitch** and tone – called an **intonation pattern**. Presenters appear to talk quite naturally, especially on informal breakfast shows, but they are acutely aware that it is easy for their voice to become monotonous. This happens when the voice tone is flat, the pace of their speech is the same over several sentences, and when the ends of sentences **fade**.

It is easy to tell that presenters and announcers work really hard at their voice production when they are compared with inexperienced listeners on phone-ins. The listeners' intonation is usually even and their pitch quite high. This is less compelling than that of a professional presenter or announcer.

Pitch											
high											
medium											
low											
	I	can't	be-lieve	I'm	on	the	ra-dio	—	I'm	so	exci-ted!

high											
medium											
low											
	I	can't	be-lieve	I'm	on	the	ra-dio	—	I'm	so	exci-ted!

Try reading these sentences aloud to a friend, following the rising and falling intonation patterns shown, but use the same noise level for each. Which pattern does your friend think is the most interesting and which the most boring? Why do you think this is so?

28

While varying intonation keeps people tuned in, research shows that there are certain voice pitch levels and particular intonation patterns that are more attractive than others. A normally low pitch level is apparently more attractive than a high one. Spoken English has a restricted set of intonation patterns but it seems that alternating between a rising and a falling ending keeps us all listening – and a presenter with a wide tonal range is more interesting than one with a narrow spectrum. In recent years there has been a trend for some reporters and presenters to end their sentences on a stressed high syllable – known as 'upspeak' in the USA. For a time this was quite popular but has become rather overused and irritating.

No second chance

We will see in the section on commercials how pre-recording allows the announcer or actor to do several **takes**, which gives them a chance to achieve the required voice control, pitch, intonation pattern and expression. Live presenters and continuity announcers have no such luxury and instead develop a set number of intonation patterns and pitch levels which they use for most situations. These have to be continually re-evaluated by the **producer** who is keen to avoid monotony. Only after a programme can these things be properly ironed out. Presenters must also keep the sound going and keep the listener glued to the station – there is never a good time to pause. This is called continuity and is a much sought-after skill among radio presenters.

Many breakfast shows have more than one presenter. It is important that they have an easy relationship with each other and can improvise at will. They are often chosen for their contrasting characters. But it is equally important that their voice quality and intonation are not too similar.

Clear delivery

Radio has affected the way we judge spoken language, and has influenced the way it is taught in our schools. 'Received Pronunciation' (RP) or standard pronunciation developed from early radio presenters' delivery which was marked by its clarity and showed no strong regional accent. This style was copied by many educators.

Acting for advertisements

Acting for radio commercials is the same as for radio drama, except that it is very concentrated. In any type of radio acting, every word, every change of the voice counts. But every tiny sound that you make is also heard!

Hearing is believing

The radio actor has to 'get into character' in just the same way as for any other medium. Many actors 'feel' each part they play using a technique known as 'method' acting. The first step in achieving this is to study every aspect of the role, really to 'live' it. This means the actors must first rid themselves of much of their own identity.

Radio commercials are so short there is little time to 'get into character'. The experienced **voice-over** actor develops a technique using short bursts of deep concentration to blot out everything else, and acquires a knack for knowing quickly what the advertiser is trying to achieve. It is rather like having a short bit-part in a film, except that in the case of commercials, the actor often has to take the listener through an entire miniature plot rather than slot the character into a much larger scenario.

Being natural

An actor has to make up for the fact that the listener cannot see facial expression or body gesture, so he or she has to find action and reaction through the voice. This does not mean overacting – in fact it takes a lot of conscious thought and control to seem 'normal' without appearing dull. But sounding like your average person-on-the-street is often exactly what advertising companies want. In a radio play, if everything sounds highly dramatic then there is no contrast – the words and the plot lose their impact and meaning. Many **directors** for commercials play safe by employing an actor with what is called a 'brown' voice, that is a steady, older male voice with friendly, confident low tones.

Studio time

It takes a whole day in the studio to rehearse and record just half an hour of a radio play. But a one-minute commercial voice-over takes very little time in proportion to this – often just a few minutes, even with several **takes**. Studio time is expensive, so every commercial will be given a production **slot** and a tight schedule to work to. Some directors even use a stopwatch! The actor usually sees the script just a few minutes before recording – there is no time to rehearse. The schedule also has to allow for pre-production time spent in setting up the studio and testing the equipment.

Working from home

Regular commercial actors have studios set up in their own homes. They link with the studio control room directly through special phone lines (called Integrated Services Digital Network or ISDN), or make pre-recorded tapes which are then mixed with sound effects and **jingles** in the post-production stage.

Radio commercial voice-overs are often recorded in sound booths. Actors can be given several scripts to reel off in just one session.

On the job

A radio actor needs a broad voice range with a strong low note, sensitivity to sound and a lot of patience! Try studying first for stage or screen acting and then get experience as an announcer on a local college or hospital radio. Finally, make a demonstration tape to send to studios and production companies. Begin with your own voice explaining who you are. Then record a few 30-second slot scripts for real products in a range of voices, none of them too extreme!

The big stage

More complex radio commercials with several actors involved are performed in a studio using several microphones. This is more like a radio play, which is a lengthy and technically more complex process, using sound effects and movement.

Moving around the mikes

Doors, drawers, cupboards and curtains are often set on wheels, to be opened or closed at the right microphone. Here, an actor or special effects technician is opening and closing a door.

In the studio, the red light is on – that is the **cue** for the first **take**. Each of the characters has their own cue light and speaks through a numbered microphone. On the script, the microphones are numbered too, against every character's lines. This shows the actors where they should position themselves. Sometimes they have to move silently from one microphone to another. At other times the underlined instructions on the script indicate that the actors' movements around the studio should be audible.

Directors usually like to rehearse and then record a scene in one particular sound set, using effects like those you can see in the picture. Then they move on to a different sound set, not necessarily in the order of the plot. This method is known as rehearse-record. Occasionally directors like to rehearse the whole performance then record it in sequence. This is called recording at-a-run.

Making a noise

If you have ever been to a pop concert you will notice that when performers speak into the mike between songs, they do not always get the smooth, crisp sound that they achieve when they are singing and playing instruments. Usually, this is because they speak right on top of the microphone, causing popping, and too loudly, causing blasting. Popping is the fluffy, fizzy sound of plosive consonants – these are the letters b, p, t, d, k and hard c. Blasting distorts the sound.

You can hear for yourself how easy it is to 'pop'. Put your mouth close to the rim of a long glass tumbler or the neck of a milk bottle and voice the plosive consonants over it. Then repeat the letters but with your mouth about four centimetres away from the rim of the glass. You will notice that the second time the consonants sound clearer and less resonant (booming).

When actors make a mistake the director does another take, which is then edited in at the post-production stage. For commercials, monologues (plays performed by just one actor) and book readings, the editor often asks for the tape to be rewound just before the fault. The actor then listens to the pitch and tempo of the piece and continues, correcting their previous mistake. This involves less work later.

The editor is responsible for making sure that all the different takes are fitted together to produce a smooth finished item. Editors often have to reduce pre-recorded items, by removing unwanted sounds or words, to ensure that they fit the required time **slot**.

Setting the scene

The live acting studio is equipped with hard screens to create live or bright sound, and soft, cloth-covered screens for dead sound. For a damped-down, outdoor effect, the studio walls are padded. Different surfaces on the floor and a set of stairs give realistic sound effects as the actor or **studio manager** moves – the surfaces can include carpet, wood, concrete and stone. Actors and special effects technicians sometimes have to dress in costume, especially in a period play. This is so that the materials rustle and flap with an authentic sound. Technicians also engage in fight scenes and perform other sounds such as turning on taps.

Making mistakes

These are some of the problems faced by radio performers:

✿ Crashing in – not allowing the previous actor to finish their lines. Some actors are too keen to bite the cue, which means to come in on their cue in good time.
✿ Going into the dead – moving out of a mono-mike's field of sound.
✿ Pitching up – copying the pitch level of a fellow-actor's voice.
✿ Rustling the script and tapping or blowing into the mike – a director's nightmare!
✿ 'Fluffing' words – the simple problem of not forming words properly.

Turn the Radio On

How does it sound?

Sound-waves are completely invisible. So how can we identify and control them? And how are they transferred from their source to their audience? Understanding how sound works is crucial not only to a radio station's technical experts but also to its **directors**, presenters and actors.

The ways of radio waves

Radio sound is communicated by equipment that changes it into electromagnetic waves, which travel in straight lines through space. Electromagnetic waves are vibrating electric and magnetic fields of force which radiate from their source. There are different bands of waves with different functions – radio waves, infra-red, visible light and so on. These are all part of the electromagnetic range, or spectrum. Radio waves can travel very long distances by means of **transmitters**. The waves are picked up by the **receiver** in your radio set, which converts the electromagnetic waves back into sound. This process describes **analogue** broadcasting.

Tuning in

Every radio station transmits on its own **frequency** – rather like a railway track for sound-waves. Different types of radio station use certain frequencies, and it is very important for a station to be available on the frequency of its choice. Of course, nothing will be heard without a radio receiver. Good quality radio sound needs a sensitive receiver to pick up the frequency.

The radio's **fidelity** should be high, which means that the receiver should respond so that all audio frequencies are amplified, or made stronger, equally. The ability to receive radio signals from one station and reject those from another on a nearby frequency is important, too. A good radio also filters out or shields unwanted noise such as hum, whistle and hiss.

Sounds different

Sound is heavily manipulated inside the studio. The way in which the voice is expressed and effects are made, how microphones are used and the nature of the space in which sound is created all affect the resulting broadcast. This does not only mean the volume of the sound but also the quality – whether it is clear or muffled, resonant (booming) or dead. Such differences are used to create a particular atmosphere, or to bring contrast to the programme. They also reveal to the listener the environment a sound is supposed to be coming from – maybe outside on a windy headland, or inside an echoing cathedral. News reporters really do broadcast live news items from such places. But if, for instance, a drama or advertisement requires the characteristics of these sound environments then they can be created very realistically, and more reliably, inside the studio, as we saw on page 32.

The first radio

Who invented radio? In the late 19th century many scientists from Europe and the USA contributed to our knowledge of radio waves and electronics – the two fields of study needed to create radio as we know it today. But many people attribute the invention of radio to the Italian electrical engineer, Guglielmo Marconi, who by 1899 had established commercial communication between the UK and France. By 1902 the first crackly radio links crossed the Atlantic from the UK to the USA.

Radio transmission masts are often very tall and vulnerable to bad weather. Many people also object to these masts being sited near their homes.

On the job

If you want to work as a sound engineer in a radio station, you will need to study sciences and mathematics at school. You then need a good grasp of electronics, sound systems, and increasingly, information technology. These can be combined in a sound engineer's course. Try working as a volunteer on a local radio station to get studio experience.

Catching the waves

Thousands of listeners have turned on their radios and tuned into the early morning show on the regular **waveband**, and the station is still there as usual. But how did the programme reach its audience? And what do all those letters and numbers on our radio sets mean?

Looking at your radio

Your radio set is a **receiver**. Basically, it reverses the process of the **transmitter** by changing back electric impulses into sound. When you turn on your radio set, you are linking it to a transmitter, often miles away. The transmitter in turn links back to the radio station. Each of these three pieces of equipment uses **antennae** or aerials to 'catch' the **frequency** of radio waves that carry the programme. And your radio set has to be tuned so that it will receive the correct frequency. But what are frequencies? What are waves?

The ionosphere is a band of gas layers wrapped around the earth's upper atmosphere. Short wavelengths can penetrate the ionosphere to reach satellite stations. From here, information can be transmitted all over the world. But the ionosphere prevents long wavelengths from reaching space, making them bounce back down to earth. This is why long wavelengths are used only to transmit information within a small area.

Radio waves, like light waves, have different lengths and speeds. They are used for different types of transmission – for your radio set, for telephone, television, radar, navigational systems and space communication. Each kind of wave travels with a kind of pulse – moving at a certain number of cycles every second, or frequency, which is how waves are measured. The shortest waves have the most cycles per second; they have the highest frequency. The longest waves have the least cycles per second, or the lowest frequency.

The cycles per second are known as hertz, and are named after the early German radio scientist, Heinrich Hertz. If you look on your radio, you might see markings such as MHz and kHz. These are two of the different cycle speeds – kHz stands for kilohertz, which run at a rate of 1000 cycles per second, and MHz stands for megahertz, which represent one million cycles per second. So kHz have a lower frequency than MHz.

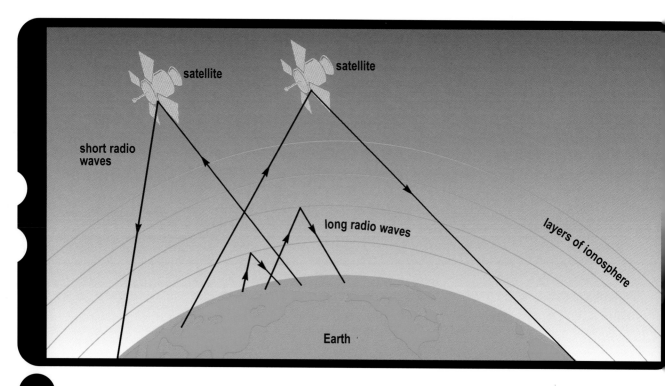

*Both terrestrial **analogue** radio and cable are difficult to receive in mountainous terrain. Apart from the mountains themselves interfering with signals, it is often too difficult to set up transmitters or lay cable. The way ahead is more broadcasting via satellite.*

A good reception

Sound-waves sent from a radio station to your set are transmitted on **carrier waves**. These are continuous electrical oscillations (vibrations) generated by transmitters. But in order to receive all the different types of sound, carrier waves have to be modulated (varied). AM and FM are two types of modulated carrier wave. AM stands for Amplitude **Modulation**, which indicates that the strength of the wave is varied in order to accept different sounds. FM stands for Frequency Modulation, which means that the frequency of the wave is varied instead.

An increasing number of stations are broadcasting on the much-favoured FM, which is more varied and also more stable than AM. AM tends to pick up more static **interference**, like the lightning storm in the picture on page 38. FM is able to reproduce different kinds of sound more faithfully than AM because its frequency range is much greater. FM, though, is usually carried on very high frequencies and very short waves, which means that they do not travel as far as AM, which is often carried on low frequencies and longer waves. To compensate for this, the transmitting antennae for FM stations often have to be very tall, in order for the signal to go as far as possible. As placing tall antennae is often very unpractical, FM stations are successfully broadcast through telephone wires or special cable – like that used for cable TV.

Hearing clearly

How does radio reach everyone? There is a limited number of **carrier waves** in the electromagnetic spectrum (see page 34), so only a limited number of stations can **transmit** programmes within a certain amount of space. How does radio manage to reach most people clearly, without **interference**?

*Radio waves can be disrupted or distorted by electrical interference – or static. Electrical storms and electrical equipment, such as **two-way radio**, car ignition systems and high-powered sewing machines that have not been properly shielded, all affect radio waves. The circuits of radios themselves should be properly shielded from external interference by a highly conductive or magnetic material.*

Technical tips

Cellular radio is a transmission system designed to make radio signals clearer and more available. It consists of a **network** of hexagonally arranged waveband 'cells', each having their own **transmitter**. As you travel, your **receiver** automatically tunes in to each in turn. Cell-phones and other personal communication systems, such as pagers and voice-mail, are used within this radio network.

Sharing the waves

The question of interference has led to each nation controlling how many stations can operate and who gets which **waveband**. Of course, you cannot legislate for other countries, which is why you can sometimes hear interference from a station belonging to the nation next door! Most nations control broadcasting through a ministry of communications. This ensures that wavebands are fairly and effectively distributed, and that a code of conduct is administered which all radio stations have to abide by. This practical government role in allocating wavebands has inevitably led to governments also being responsible for regulating the industry in terms of programme content and allowing certain stations to broadcast.

A rigid control of wavebands ensures that reception is clear for all radio stations. In countries such as the USA, where there are thousands of radio stations, it is very important to stick strictly within the bandwidth limit. A deviation of just a hundredth of one per cent causes serious interference with even distant stations on the same **frequency**.

A larger audience

Most local and national radio stations hope to be granted FM waves wherever their programmes are transmitted. The number of listeners to the BBC World Service rose from 143 million in 1999 to 151 million in 2000. The increase is attributed to the station changing some of its transmission from AM to local FM, which has made reception clearer and available to a wider audience. It is now also broadcast on the Internet.

The radio microphone carried by this presenter has its own transmitter fitted inside a small box and worn around the waist. The radio transmitter enables the presenter to walk around freely without being restricted by cable.

Useful radio

Radio has enabled some instruments to operate more precisely, conveniently or efficiently. The radio compass uses radio waves to find directions. And the radio pill is a miniature radio transmitter enclosed in a tiny capsule. When swallowed it sends out information about what is going on inside the body. Radio telescopes give us an idea of the shape of objects in space by picking up radio waves emitted from them.

You can't say that!

The early morning show is a seamless concoction of music, news and views. But are all the listeners happy about what they hear? It is difficult for a show packed with opinion not to offend at least one listener. What happens when it does?

Is it right? Is it fair?

Broadcasting authorities throughout the world regulate most aspects of radio transmission. They range from the number of stations that any one company can own, through the proportion of commercials that can be **transmitted**, to the extent to which owners of stations and journalists can air their own views. Most countries, too, operate policies and invoke laws on fairness, equality, decency, taste, swearing, sex and violence. These try to ensure that the listener is not offended by anything that they hear, and that young people will be protected from themes that are too adult in their content.

Each station is responsible for complying with these laws and usually has specialist media and **libel** lawyers at hand if a programme is in danger of making statements that hover on the edge of legality. Breaking the regulations can mean a fine or even the removal of the station's licence. Broadcasting regulations, though, often conflict with a country's laws on freedom of speech.

Listeners keep radio stations alive and it is against the interests of a station not to respond to their complaints. But, sometimes, a station has to choose between keeping listeners who tune in specifically for the sensationalism, or keeping those who object to it.

Making a complaint

What happens if listeners hear something on the radio that they find offensive? How do they complain? The first course of action is to contact the radio station. Most stations broadcast a **slot** that allows listeners to express their opinion on the programmes, either in writing or through a phone-in. Large stations also have a complaints unit that will answer queries individually. Failing that, listeners can contact the national broadcasting standards commission or separate radio authority. Some countries operate different complaints authorities for publicly-financed and commercial broadcasting. There is usually a separate organization, too, for monitoring advertising standards, ensuring that their guidelines have not been breached. Media magazines usually carry the names and addresses of these agencies as well as the week's programme listings.

One form of free speech not allowed in the majority of countries is that of using someone's name or voice for personal gain. In radio this applies particularly to impersonations in commercials, which is why it is essential for all actors and presenters to develop their own voice and style.

*Heated political debate before elections is good for both politicians and **ratings**! In the USA, during the 1930s, President Roosevelt made regular broadcasts to the nation outlining his policies. These 'fireside chats' and his calm, friendly tone increased his popularity.*

Discrimination

In radio broadcasting we can see no gender, no colour, no race and no creed – yet through the voice we can still detect many of these aspects of humankind. And while in the USA and Europe white women have managed to carve out careers in radio presentation, and even production, quite early on in the history of radio, their black and Asian counterparts have had to wait. Until the 1970s, their role was restricted largely to entertainment, often playing **stereotypes**. But through equal opportunity laws and local ethnic minority broadcasting, presenters, **producers** and **directors** have emerged and they and their views are now better represented at national level.

The verdict

So what do listeners think of their early morning radio show? How do the rest of the media respond to it? Through reviews and **ratings** the **producer** and the owner of a station learn whether they have got the right formula.

What did they think?

'The audience is the final actor' is a common saying in the media and entertainment world. In radio it refers to the fact that the response of the public is an interaction – a way of participating in a show and of shaping its future, for in turn, radio stations will react to the public's response. One of the most pressing issues is knowing what to change, when to change it, or even if change is necessary at all. It is so easy for the listener to find a station that keeps up more with the times than their regular station, or one that has not altered so much that it has lost its original appeal.

Market researchers ask about a listener's age group, social and economic bracket and general tastes as well as his or her listening habits. This gives them an idea of the profile of their average listener. Radio stations cannot afford to upset their listener base but at the same time need to know if it is changing, and why.

Finding out what listeners think of the programme is crucial for both the station and advertisers. So both conduct surveys using telephone questionnaires and focus groups, among other techniques. They also take very careful consideration of any points raised through phone-ins and letters.

Local radio stations and advertisers can take samplings by locating listeners via local telephone directories and electoral registers. Local radio **networks** combine the results to find out which programmes work best in certain regions. National radio, with its vast resources, can use a wider range of sampling techniques or can employ ratings companies to assess the success or failure of stations, presenters, particular programmes or even small **slots** within them. In the USA, the larger media companies use well-established organizations such as Nielsen Ratings. But Internet radio listeners might find their listening habits silently monitored by agencies using **digital** technology to find out their tastes and therefore the kinds of advertisements they can ply them with. There are serious privacy issues concerning these techniques.

Very public opinion

Last, but by no means least, what did the reviewers think? A new local radio show can expect to receive a comment in the media column of their local newspaper, but a national radio station breakfast show will find reviews in national newspapers and media magazines. These same publications, both local and national, will also be represented at the major award ceremonies for radio **producers**, **directors** and presenters. So, too, will electronics manufacturers, such as Sony. Otherwise, radio prizes are usually tucked behind more prestigious media at what are really newspaper press, television and film award ceremonies. That is, unless they are rewarded in the USA, where the prestigious annual Silver Microphone Awards acknowledge programme-makers and advertising agencies working only in local and state radio. The categories range from 'best use of humour' in an advertisement to the 'best broadcast non-English programme' for ethnic minority listeners.

Radio awards ceremonies have been criticized for giving out prizes to the same presenters and production teams again and again. The names of presenters in particular, and especially DJs, crop up regularly as winners. But this should not be a surprise, as many well-known radio personalities stay in the business for several decades, their charisma earning good ratings for the radio stations they work for. The elite, especially those working on **prime-time** breakfast shows, work very hard at keeping their voice fresh without losing their original attraction. It is this balance of trying to lure new listeners, and yet not lose all of the old ones, that keeps presenters, producers and **station managers** permanently on their toes.

Alistair Cooke

What lasts in radio? Who lasts? If Alistair Cooke is anything to go by, American anecdotes and news items picking out the quirky and the quaint are a winning formula. Although now a citizen of the USA, Alistair Cooke has sent his weekly 'Letter from America' across the waves to his native Britain and all over the world for over 50 years. Radio still produces a core of high-profile writers, presenters and DJs. Their legacy often lies in the catch-phrases they have coined, which linger on in our language.

The future

No one knows how **prime-time** radio will develop. Its trends will doubtless run parallel to the ever-changing needs of busy people the world over. Radio's future also rests on its making use of technological advances in the **digital** age and the opening up of space.

Radio for all

The continuation of nationally controlled and financed radio stations enables the majority of people world-wide to have easy access to information and entertainment. Satellite communications have also allowed the numbers of small stations and amateur radio to grow, ensuring that minority interests are well served and that radio stays alive and accessible to all. Since the 1960s, radio satellites have opened up the waves to amateur **transmissions**. Known as Oscar (Orbiting Satellites Carrying Amateur Radio), these have ridden 'piggyback' on major communication satellites for nearly 40 years. But it is the Internet that has transformed radio since the mid-1990s ...

Internet radio shows have become increasingly popular, which in time will probably lead to the creation of an international breakfast show **format**. The Internet is being used more and more for interactive radio shows and their website spin-offs, expanding the function of radio with on-line gimmicks such as quizzes and scratch cards. On-line presenters can now integrate an almost infinite amount of Internet information into their shows. With no need for commercial breaks, over 90 per cent of an Internet radio show can be dedicated to music or chat.

Eliot Stein is already beginning to influence breakfast shows with his softer style. In 2000, the UK's prestigious BBC Radio One pop music breakfast show formally dropped the 'zoo' format and began to include more serious news items.

America's Eliot Stein is the pioneer of the on-line talk show, which he set up in 1994. But in the early days you had to tap into the chat, for the programme was in text only. In 1996, Stein launched the first live audible show, creating a forum for topical discussion. Unlike the 'zoo' formula described on page 7, his **slots** are non-confrontational, allowing information-sharing rather than trying to increase the **ratings** with public show-downs and pranks.

HOLLYWOOD HOTLINE™

Since 1982 -- The World's First And Oldest Interactive Entertainment Service

Click here to read about the history of Hollywood Hotline™

You've Read And Heard Our Entertainment News, Movie Reviews, Celebrity Interviews, And Other Features Since 1982 All Over America Online, Compuserve, On Prodigy, National Magazines And Newspapers, And More

COMING IN NOVEMBER:
"HOLLYWOOD HOTLINE™ WITH ELIOT STEIN"

DAILY LIVE AUDIO/INTERACTIVE TEXT INTERVIEW SHOW
featuring celebrities, industry personnel, creative folks, authors, experts
on MOVIES, TV, MUSIC, NEW MEDIA AND MORE!

HOLLYWOOD HOTLINE ™ IS A REGISTERED TRADEMARK IN THE UNITED STATES PATENT AND TRADEMARK OFFICE

Ordinary mobile phones now have Internet links for radio phone-in items and portable on-line sets with screens (called WAPs). But it is an exclusive technology, available only to rich nations or the few wealthy members of poor ones. It is a luxury for people in some countries, where the Net is still not free.

Free radio?

Millions of people across the globe have no access to a reliable source of electricity, nor money for batteries. The whole of humankind faces the possibility of dwindling energy resources and the ever-increasing problem of battery disposal. Inventions such as the BayGen Freeplay radio (see also page 8) provide practical technology for a more environmentally friendly future.

This BayGen Freeplay radio has a clockwork mechanism inside that generates and stores enough electricity for around one hour's listening after a 30-second windup. Some BayGen Freeplays are now also solar-powered.

Technical tips

☆ One of the latest broadcasting techniques involves converting radio waves into a computerized form. This is known as digital transmission and it is easier to control and manipulate than **analogue** (see page 34). Digital transmission can be broadcast on very high frequencies (see page 37). It also takes up less transmission space than analogue.

☆ An analogue-to-digital (A/D) converter is an integrated circuit (a microchip) which allows a digital computer to accept data from an analogue device. The A/D converter is also called a digitizer. Sound in digital form is more stable than its analogue counterpart.

Glossary

air time   the time allowed for a particular broadcast to take place, whether it is a programme, commercial or other slot

analogue   sound that is translated into radio waves by a radio station's transmitter, and then translated back to sound inside the radio set

antenna   (or aerial) a structure for sending out and receiving sound signals

audio technician   technician that makes sure that sound equipment in a radio station works properly

carrier wave   wave generated by a transmitter to carry sound-waves sent out by a radio station

continuity   to be without breaks or pauses. A radio announcer who links programmes and introduces items and slots is called a continuity announcer.

cue   1) signal to the presenter to begin a new slot or action. 2) To set music and so on, in readiness to play it.

democratic   country with a government elected by its people

digital   radio waves that are converted into a computerized form for transmission, making them more stable and enabling more to be transmitted at one time

director   a progamme coordinator (also sometimes producer)

drive time   the hours during which most people travel to and from work or school

fade   when one sound is gradually made quieter to be replaced by another sound

fader   slider on a radio console that brings sounds in, takes them out and fades their volume up and down

fidelity   accuracy of the balance achieved by a radio receiver when it amplifies the different frequencies

format   the way a radio show is arranged in terms of content

freelance   someone who works for different employers, usually on individual jobs or on a short-term basis

frequency   pulse of a radio wave moving at a certain number of cycles per second

interference   the disturbance of a sound signal; making unwanted noise

intonation pattern   rise and fall of a person's voice as they speak

jingle   short burst of music or song that is part of a commercial or which introduces a presenter or slot

libel to broadcast untrue and damaging information about a person or organization

modulation varying a radio wave so that it can carry sound

narrowcasting radio station that broadcasts specialized programmes for a particular interest group

network group of radio stations that share programmes

pitch level of a person's voice, whether high, medium or low

prime time morning and early evening peak listening times

producer programme coordinator (also sometimes director)

ratings calculation of the size of audience for each radio show

receiver equipment that receives sound signals, such as radio

revenue income, or money

signature tune tune that introduces a programme or a slot

slot 1) scheduled item in a radio show – a quiz, commercial, phone-in, and so on. 2) Space in a schedule to be filled with programmes and items.

station manager person in charge of a radio station's finances and also the day-to-day output of the station

stereotype a fixed, and often not very positive image of a person or group of people

studio manager (SM) radio station's technical supervisor

take a recording

trail the broadcast of a short section of a future programme or item, designed to encourage listeners to tune into it later

transmit to broadcast a programme

transmitter equipment that produces, modulates and sends out radio signals

two-way radio radio sets with microphones that enable people to communicate with each other

voice-over spoken part of a pre-recorded commercial

waveband range of wavelengths between two given limits, allocated to radio stations

Index

Titles in the *Behind Media* series include:

| Hardback | 0 431 11450 1 |

| Hardback | 0 431 11452 8 |

| Hardback | 0 431 11463 3 |

| Hardback | 0 431 11461 7 |

| Hardback | 0 431 11460 9 |

| Hardback | 0 431 11462 5 |

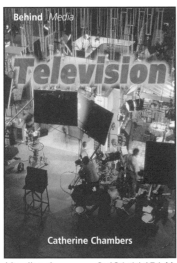

| Hardback | 0 431 11451 X |

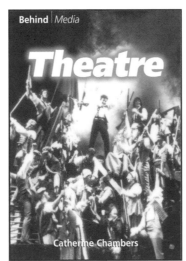

| Hardback | 0 431 11453 6 |

Find out about other Heinemann books on our website www.heinemann.co.uk/library